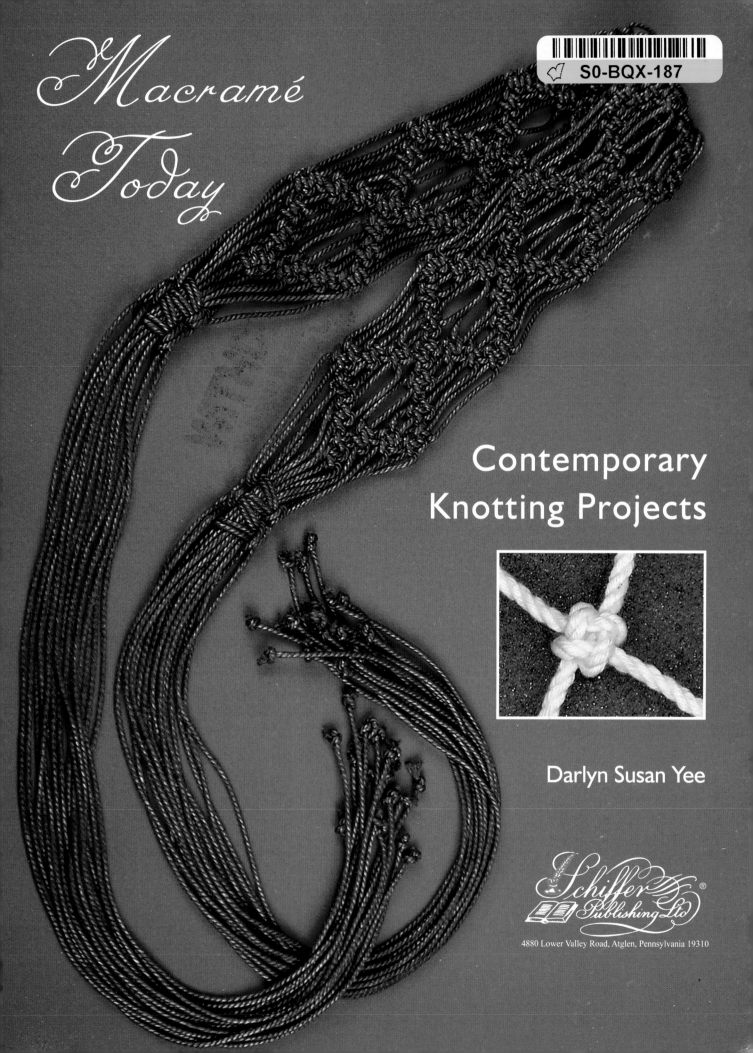

# Macramé Today

## Contemporary Knotting Projects

Darlyn Susan Yee

Schiffer Publishing Ltd
4880 Lower Valley Road, Atglen, Pennsylvania 19310

# Dedication

For my parents,
who started me on the right path
to become the person I am.

And for my husband,
who encourages my continued growth,
both as an artist and as a person.


"All of life is a journey.
Which paths we take,
what we look back on,
and what we look forward to is up to us.
We determine our destination,
what kind of road we take and
how happy we are when we get there."

*– Anonymous*

**Other Schiffer Books on Related Subjects:**
*The Stitches of Creative Embriodery*. Jacqueline
    Enthoven. ISBN: 978-0-88740-111-4. $24.99
*Dyeing Wool: 20 Techniques, Beginner to Advanced*.
    Karen Schellinger. ISBN: 978-0-7643-3432-0. $59.99
*Color and Fiber*. Lambert, Staepelaer, Fry. ISBN: 978-0-
    88740-065-05. $49.99


Copyright © 2011 by Darlyn Susan Yee

Library of Congress Control Number: 2011927263

Designed by Stephanie Daugherty
Type set in Miss Fajardose/Zurich BT
ISBN: 978-0-7643-3799-4
Printed in China

Schiffer Books are available at special discounts for bulk purchases for sales promotions or premiums. Special editions, including personalized covers, corporate imprints, and excerpts can be created in large quantities for special needs. For more information contact the publisher:

Published by Schiffer Publishing Ltd.
4880 Lower Valley Road
Atglen, PA 19310
Phone: (610) 593-1777; Fax: (610) 593-2002
E-mail: Info@schifferbooks.com

For the largest selection of fine reference books on this and related subjects, please visit our website at **www. schifferbooks.com**
We are always looking for people to write books on new and related subjects. If you have an idea for a book please contact us at the above address.


This book may be purchased from the publisher.
Include $5.00 for shipping.
Please try your bookstore first.
You may write for a free catalog.
In Europe, Schiffer books are distributed by
Bushwood Books
6 Marksbury Ave.
Kew Gardens
Surrey TW9 4JF England
Phone: 44 (0) 20 8392 8585; Fax: 44 (0) 20 8392 9876
E-mail: info@bushwoodbooks.co.uk
Website: www.bushwoodbooks.co.uk

# Contents

# Foreword

Fiber art, one of mankind's earliest art forms, is a diverse label referring to any artistic technique that involves the joining of fibrous materials. Fiber arts initially arose from necessity: a need to provide shelter, to protect the body from the cold, or to contain or transport food. Early fiber arts were rooted in community and collectivism, as they underscored social and familial ties, particularly for women. As the art forms progressed, more sophisticated techniques were developed and various found materials began to be incorporated into the designs. From this, fiber arts were no longer simply functional wares, but also became status symbols and precious objects as well.

Contemporary artists are looking for ways to reposition the fiber arts in art criticism and scholarship by reinforcing its legitimacy as a viable form of personal and artistic expression. Darlyn Susan Yee is one such artist, who is redefining the art of macramé. Macramé has its origins in the thirteenth century Middle East (the Arabic word *migramah* translates to "ornamental fringe or veil"). It is an art form that consists of knotting and tying fiber, which results in a complex blend of texture and intricate pattern (usually geometric).

Today's macramé artists are experimenting with materials and techniques to create entirely new ways for the viewer to consider and interact with fiber. These innovative forms derive from a contemporary context, while simultaneously acknowledging their traditions and origins. Such practices are a tacit acknowledgement of the lineage of macramé, where the past informs the present, and the present will invariably inform the future. Yee's work indicates that she is aware of this strong relationship between the past and present. While her work clearly communicates to the viewer in a contemporary vocabulary, there are slight underlying references to some of the more traditional features of macramé (and the fiber arts in general).

Encouraging a complete consideration of the versatility of macramé, Yee presents her work in various ways. Some are freestanding sculpture; others are kinetic, curvilinear compositions suspended in air. Some of her work is mounted onto two-dimensional surfaces to contrast the three-dimensionality of the macramé object. One noteworthy feature of Yee's work is the transformation of practical objects into works of visual art intended for display. Many of her sculptural pieces take the form of a vessel, which initially brings to mind the function of containment. However, with the macramé technique, the vessel is made of knotted fibers which create a surface with open areas of space. Thus, its functional potential is quite limited and is therefore subjugated to its aesthetic qualities.

The working process of macramé is painstaking: many of Yee's pieces contain thousands of knots. With such a labor intensive technique, the process of making the work becomes just as important as its end result. There is also a certain intimacy in Yee's work which comes from working with macramé. To completely understand and appreciate the visual intricacies of the technique, the viewer must form a personal relationship with the work by being in close proximity. Each of the small knots reminds the viewer that at one point Yee too was just as close to the work. This creates an intimacy shared by artist and viewer that is divided by time and space. It is also in this close proximity that the viewer comes to the realization that there is something of Yee herself that is laid bare in the work. Secured within each knot is an expression of self and the remnants personal meditation. The expression embedded in each knot is tightly bound to another. These small, disparate parts are then linked together to create a cohesive, unified whole.

The work of Darlyn Susan Yee does much to progress the development and evolution of macramé. She successfully reconciles its aesthetics (a simple, raw, unassuming beauty) with the contemporary experience in a way that is inventive and relevant. In the spirit of contemporary art's experimentation with material, Yee's reevaluation of the physical qualities of fiber do much to undermine the restrictive stylistic and categorical labels that artists have been actively deconstructing since the end of the postmodern period.

Brandelyn Dillaway
Gallery Director and Associate Faculty
Mt. San Jacinto College

# Preface

This book is a direct result of making choices as opportunities materialized. It is a summary of the knowledge I have acquired to date. There is more information out there, and I encourage you to seek it and to forge your own path with the knowledge you acquire.

When I learned the basic knots that are discussed in this book, I was nine years old at summer day camp. I made the requisite owl pendant and belt of the time period. From that point on, however, string and rope were never the same when I got through with them. I never felt fully challenged or satisfied by following patterns. I worked on the fly and created my own unique projects: guitar straps for teachers and friends, embellishments on my clothing, and wall and window décor for my apartment.

As an adult, I dabbled with displaying my work at the craft cooperatives and began entering some of my work in the home arts and hobby divisions of county and state fairs. These activities resulted in viewer feedback and a stronger sense of where my skills were in relation to others.

I then challenged myself to create more sculptural knotted works, which I began entering in local and national visual arts competitions. I joined cooperative fine art galleries and have been exhibiting my work steadily in fine art contexts ever since. I've won a number of awards, and each exhibition has led me to another opportunity or two to pursue.

As a member of TAG Gallery in Santa Monica, California, the opportunity arose to submit work for a publication. I was one of five TAG Gallery artists chosen by Tina Skinner for inclusion in *100 Artists of the West Coast II* from Schiffer Publishing. Not long after, I was approached to write this book.

The process of creating this book has led me to examine my passion for knotting under a microscope. I had never had reason to review the how and why of what I do. Experimentation with other mediums has expanded my knowledge of material and process. But I always come back to knotting. Fiber feels so much warmer and friendlier than clay in my hands. I'm comforted by the warm weight of the yarn or string splayed out on my lap as I work. The variations in texture and perceived color that can be created with knot patterns continue to excite me.

The knots seem to tie themselves when I get into the groove; for me it is almost a meditative process. One afternoon I realized that I wasn't looking as I worked and the knots were just as even as the ones before them.

May your journey through the projects in this book inspire you to forge your own path and do more than you ever thought possible.

# Historical and Cultural Relevance

## Arabic Origin of Macramé

Macramé is an ancient form of knotting that generally is done in geometric patterns to create any number of wearable, decorative or functional items. Although earlier examples of hand knotted work exist, the origin of the term "macramé" is Arabic, meaning "fringe," and dates back to the thirteenth century. Arabian weavers would knot the extra fiber, or fringe, at the edges of loomed fabric.

## Sailor's Knotting

In the fourteenth and fifteenth centuries, macramé became popular on French and Italian ships. Intricate rope work was used to make small protective and ornamental items while at sea. Cotton and hemp cord or rope was generally chosen for their strength, durability and availability. Rails, spars and riggings were often protected by wrappings constructed in various macramé styles. Slippery decks were fitted with knotted mats for added traction.

## Religious and Regal Adornments

Athough geometric knotting patterns fell out of general popularity, macramé could be found in churches and convents adorning vestments and altar cloths. The adornments are depicted in Renaissance paintings. Macramé became a royal pastime in the seventeenth century in Western Europe. Court dress during the reign of Louis XXIV of France included silk scarves and stoles with long fringes created with this intricate knotting technique.

## Victorian Arts

During a revival of macramé in the Victorian era (1840-1900) a popular indoor occupation of the elite was decorative needlework. To demonstrate the wealth of their husbands, ladies would create intricate lace items to embellish pen cases, gas lamp brackets and curtain rails, linens, bonnets and blouses. The types of lacework included embroidery on linen, silk and velvet, tapestry, cross-stitch, tatting, lace work, netting, trimmings such as tassels, appliqué work and sewing of monograms on household linens.

## 1960s and 1970s Rediscovery

Macramé was again revived as alternative adornment in the nineteen sixties, with the hippie and peace movements. Especially in the United States, the concepts of rejecting middle-class materialism, returning to nature, and simplifying life were prevalent. All classes embraced macramé, with jewelry, belts, purses and plant hangers becoming popular items to create. Some artisans created purely decorative wall hangings and baskets, contributing their talents to the fiber art movement.

## Recurring Focus on Wearable Art

Today, macramé has regained its immense popularity. Designers on the popular television show *Project Runway* created surfwear using macramé elements.

Updated 1960s and 1970s style belts are frequently seen on ready-to-wear pants today. Knotted embellishments on t-shirts and casual wear are again available to the mass market.

Jewelry artisans have popularized micro-macramé by not just reworking patterns from the 1960s and 1970s in finer gauge thread, but also by creating innovative new patterns.

## Presence in Contemporary Art

Jane Sauer's knotted artworks are in the collections of the Smithsonian American Art Museum, and the Museum of Arts and Design.

Diane Itter's knotted work from the 1970s is also in the collection of the Museum of Arts and Design, and is referenced in the Metropolitan Museum of Art's *Heilbrunn Timeline of Art History*.

Amanda Ross-Ho references the silhouettes of macramé objects in her works carved from sheetrock or cut from painted black canvas drop cloths. These works have been displayed at the Saatchi Gallery in London and the Whitney Biennial in New York.

Angie Harbin creates coral-like structures and vessels through delicate knotting of waxed linen cords.

Galit Mastai was commissioned to make seventy huge, 1970s-inspired, wall hangings for six new Aritzia stores that opened in Canada and the United States in 2010. She has also incorporated knotted fiber work into some of her recent gold jewelry designs.

Jolanta Surma is an emerging artist exhibiting macramé hangings and sculptures in Poland. She works with natural colored jute, then hand paints each piece with watercolors.

# Tools and Supplies

Macramé can be an easy and inexpensive fiber method because there are no required tools; the supplies discussed in this chapter are suggestions, not necessities. And you'll find that certain combinations of tools work better for some projects than for others. Before you begin a project, refer to this section and consider the items you have on hand. Improvise if there is another tool or method that achieves the same end result.

## Working Surfaces

The working surface provides a firm enough place to pin your project. This will help you to keep the knots uniform in size and tension. An added benefit is that work on your project can be stopped and resumed as needed, and your project becomes more portable.

A quilter's blocking board performs multiple functions serving as: a ruler, a support for your

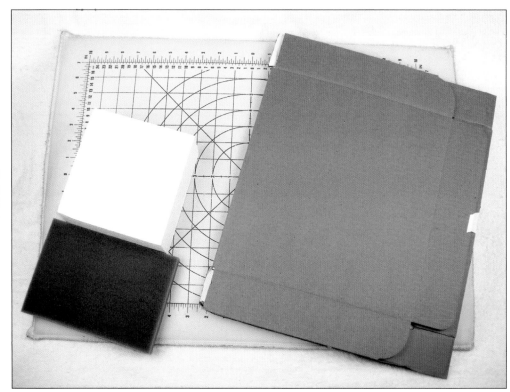

Suitable working surfaces include foam rubber, polystyrene, quilter's blocking board and cardboard.

work, and a visual reference to keep even your work in progress. Blocking board is readily available through sewing and craft retailers; it consists of a durable, pin-through board that is padded and covered in a fabric, much like an ironing board cover.

Other options for working surfaces you may have on hand are: foam rubber, polystyrene, or cardboard. Consider asking your local fabric store for a cardboard fabric bolt that they have designated for the trash.

## Pins

The pins will act as an extra set of hands, holding your project neatly to the working surface. You will find it easier to apply even tension as you work when the finished portion is held securely in position. The even tension will result in cleaner, more precise looking knots. T-pins offer the firmest support for heavier and larger projects. Quilt and Corsage pins are less visually distracting and their slender profile is more suitable for finer materials. Safety pins can be helpful for smaller projects and those you intend to transport while in-progress.

## Needles

Although not necessary to create macramé projects, needles are quite useful when you are joining or piecing finished parts of your project. Curved upholstery needles and doll needles are helpful when you need to add or move cord into a tight area of existing work. Yarn or crewel needles can also help you to adjust or remove an imperfect knot. Sail needles are especially helpful because the flat area toward the front provides a good grip when pulling cords through tight spaces.

## Cutting Implements

Any sharp scissors will be sufficient. Fabric shears are nice because they are designed to cut fibers more easily. Small craft scissors are a great choice for projects that require portability. The shapes of cuticle scissors or wire snips are handy when you need to cut very close to the surface of your knotted work.

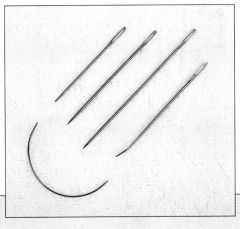

Also helpful are various specialty needles including yarn, crewel, doll, sail and curved upholstery needles.

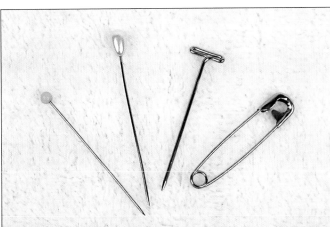

Quilt pins, corsage pins, T-pins and safety pins can secure the knotting to the board to help you to maintain even tension.

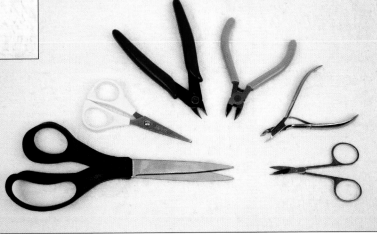

Fabric and craft scissors, wire snips, or cuticle nippers and scissors will handle all of your cutting needs.

## Holding Tools

Knotting pliers are definitely useful when you are straightening or untying a series of knots. They also work well for setting knots tight against a prior row. Needle-nosed and jeweler's pliers can provide the same benefits even though their shapes differ. Care should be taken to avoid abrading and fraying the fiber with the metal of the pliers.

Knotting pliers are especially useful, but needle nosed or jeweler's pliers will also help you with knots in tight spaces.

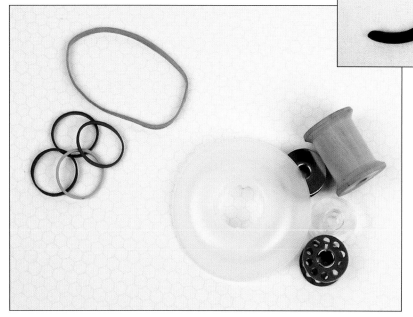

Rubber bands, spools and bobbins make ideal bundling aids for longer cords. And graph paper can be a helpful as you plan a project.

## Bundling Aids

When tackling the larger projects, you may find it helpful to gather working ends of your project material using rubber bands or attaching them onto spools or bobbins. Rubber bands are inexpensive and available in various sizes to suit your project and fiber. They come in various colors, making it easy to handle large bundles and organize sections of working cords. Spools and bobbins can also serve these purposes, but they may add weight and bulk to your work in-progress.

## Planning Aids

Should you decide to design your own projects, you might find it helpful to plan or document them on graph paper. Both hexagonal and isometric graph papers work well for this purpose, and they are available online as free downloads through a number of sources. Both designs provide plenty of diagonal reference points to guide you as you map projects that combine various knots.

# Choosing Fiber for a Project

## Strength

For a project that will be used daily, you will want to consider the durability and strength of the fiber. Consider the amount of strain you will place on the item and how the item will look after wear or use.

Fiber composition is a factor that contributes to the strength of the cord. Jute, hemp, leather and nylon are inherently strong fibers, so they will withstand a the strain of weight and wear.

Generally, a braided cord will be stronger that a twisted cord. Braided cords often consist of a braided casing over a core of another material. Twisted cords will be stronger if they are multiple ply (or section) than single ply.

In multiple ply cord, confirm that the twist of each ply runs in the opposite direction from the twist of all ply together. This will make for a more stable twisted cord that won't unravel or lengthen as you work with it.

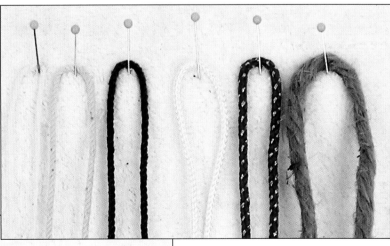

Cotton bundling or kitchen twine, cotton cable cords, nylon braided cords and jute cord.

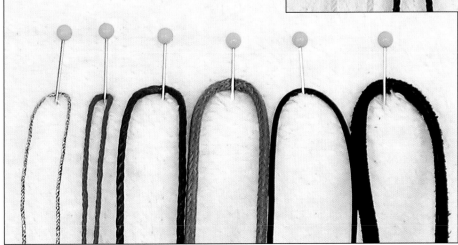

Metallic and cotton embroidery flosses, twisted and braided waxed cotton cords, faux leather and genuine leather cords.

Cotton and acrylic yarns of varying weights and knitted cords.

## Flexibility

If you are making an article of clothing, you will generally want to choose a more flexible fiber to allow it to drape gently against the body. Conversely, if you are making a more protective or durable item, you will want to choose a fiber that knots into a more rigid state.

Along with the flexibility comes slip. Some fibers, like nylon and satin cording can be so overly flexible and slippery that the knots may slide undone. Often, a multiple ply cord with opposing twist will create enough friction, or tooth, to hold the knots in place regardless of the fiber.

## Comfort

Generally, you will want to choose fiber that feels good against the skin. Some jute, hemp and metallic fibers will abrade your hands as you work on your projects. Also consider also how the finished product will feel. For example, you will want a relatively smooth fiber for sandal straps to avoid blisters from the repeat movement as you walk.

## Care

Consider whether the item you are creating is likely to pick up dirt, or will require frequent washing. If so, synthetic fibers such as nylon, acrylic, and polyamide could be among your best choices. Cotton and is also very washable, but the item may shrink slightly if it is not blocked during the drying process.

Generally speaking, you would care for any macramé item just as you would care for a hand knit item. Hand wash, block, spot treat, or dry clean according to the guidelines for the fiber used in the project.

## Visual Attributes

Some fibers are available in a wide array of colors. If you intend to dye the fiber yourself, there are great alternatives available to yarn dye or piece dye both natural and synthetic fibers. These dyes are readily available in sewing and art supply stores, and through online outlets. Diameter or width can also be a factor. If you intend to adorn the project with beads, you will need to confirm that the size of the holes in the beads you have chosen will be large enough to accept your cord.

Consider also the scale of the knots for the project. It is unlikely that you would choose rope to create a dainty knotted necklace. Nor would you be likely to choose embroidery floss to create a large shopping tote.

When possible, also consider the number of inline splices or slubs in the fiber. If you try to work with a fiber with these lumps and bumps, they will invariably fall in a spot that is difficult to conceal. You will be wise to exclude cords that contain these lumps and bumps. While measuring and cutting cords for your project, just set the spliced cords aside for a later project or for test material.

# 4

## Preparing to Work

## Measuring

To measure the length of the yarn that you will need for your work, the length of thread, yarn or cord must be at least four times longer than the piece you want to create. If you double your thread when mounting, the length must be at least eight times more.

Keep in mind that the thread length depends on which knots and how many of them you plan to use because some will expend more thread than others. Also, the thicker the thread you use, the more length you'll need. Those who are experienced in knotting procedures agree that it is always better to have cord leftover than to run out before completing your project.

When you have a general plan of a project in mind, but are not working from a pattern, consider measuring twelve to sixteen times the desired length of your finished piece. You will then be certain to have enough cord to compensate for any change in your overall plan as you work.

Any leftover materials should be saved for later use in a smaller project, or for use as test material. Upon completion of your project, place the leftovers neatly in a container or bag. Labeling for fiber content, shortest length and number of strands while the information is fresh in your mind will save time later because you will be able to see at a glance what you have on hand.

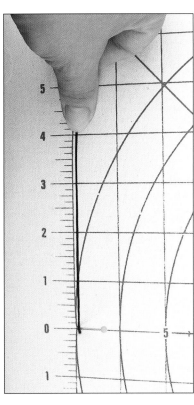

Measuring the thread or cord is the first step toward success with your project.

## Bundling or Wrapping

When working with thread, cord or yarn that is arm's length or longer, you may find it helpful to bundle or wrap the excess. You can also use rubber bands or spools, but they are not necessary.

**Method One:**
1. Hold the end of the end of the cord in one hand.
2. With the other hand, wrap the cord repeatedly around your palm.
3. Slide the bundle off your hand.
4. Form a loop around the resulting bundle.

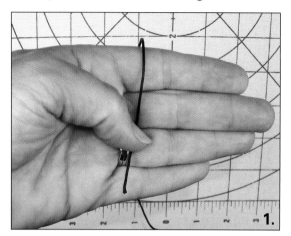

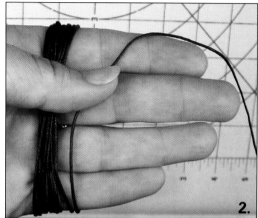

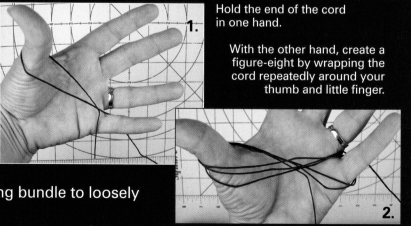

**Method Two:**
1. Hold the end of the cord in one hand.
2. With your other hand, create a figure-eight by wrapping the cord repeatedly around your thumb and little finger.
3. Slide the bundle off your hand.
4. Form a loop around the resulting bundle to loosely secure.

Hold the end of the cord in one hand.

With the other hand, create a figure-eight by wrapping the cord repeatedly around your thumb and little finger.

# Tying the Basic Knots

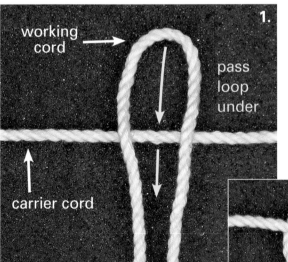

## Lark's Head

Most commonly used to loosely attach a working cord.

Provides clean consistent edge.

Other names for this knot are based upon functional use, for example: girth, strap, cow or lanyard hitch.

**Directions:**

1. Find the middle of a cord and lay a loop over a carrier cord.
2. Pass the loop behind the carrier cord.
3. Pass the free ends of the working cord through the loop and pull to tighten.

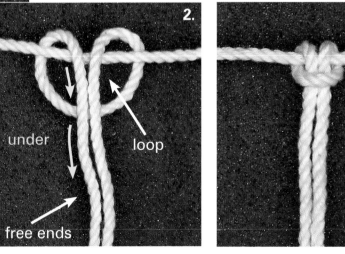

# Overhand Knot

Often used to finish ends of cord to guard
against fraying.
Also works well to secure inline beads, or to add
texture and interest instead of a bead.

### Directions:

1. Wrap the cord around itself.
2. Pass one end through.
3. Then pull tight to complete the knot.

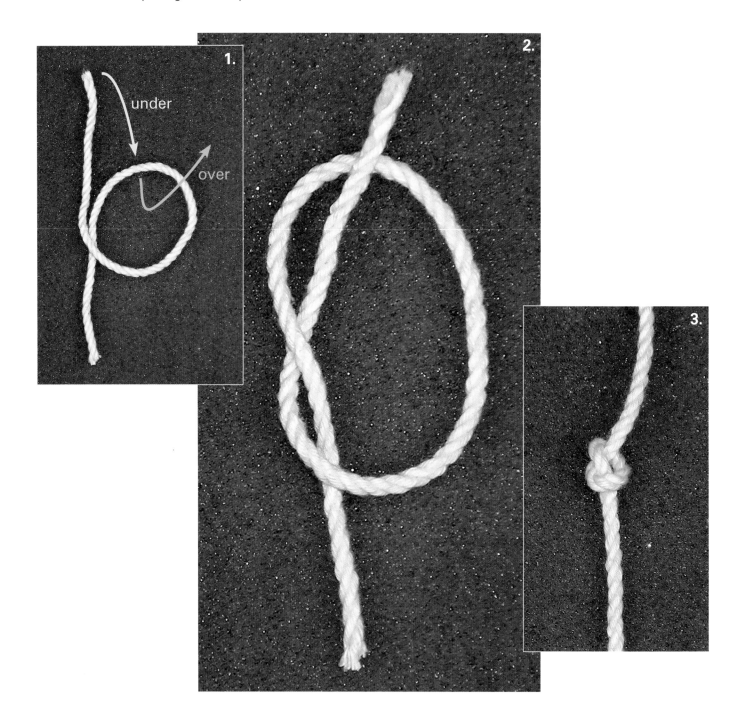

# Double Overhand Knot

The double overhand knot is bulkier than the overhand knot.

It is very difficult to untie once it has been pulled tight.

Another name, bloodknot, originated when the knot was used at the end of a whip.

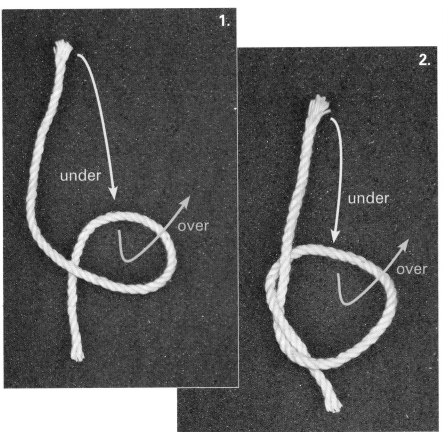

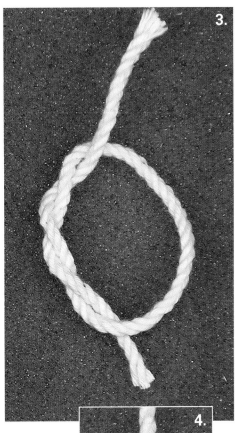

**Directions:**
1. Wrap the cord around itself.
2. Pass one end through.
3. Pass the end through a second time.
4. Then pull tight to complete the knot.

# Half Hitch

This knot is similar in structure to an overhand
knot.
It is frequently worked over a stationary cord,
or mounting dowel.

### Directions:

1. Make a loop, crossing the short or free
end under the main length of cord.
2. Bring the short end through the hole,
then down and pull.

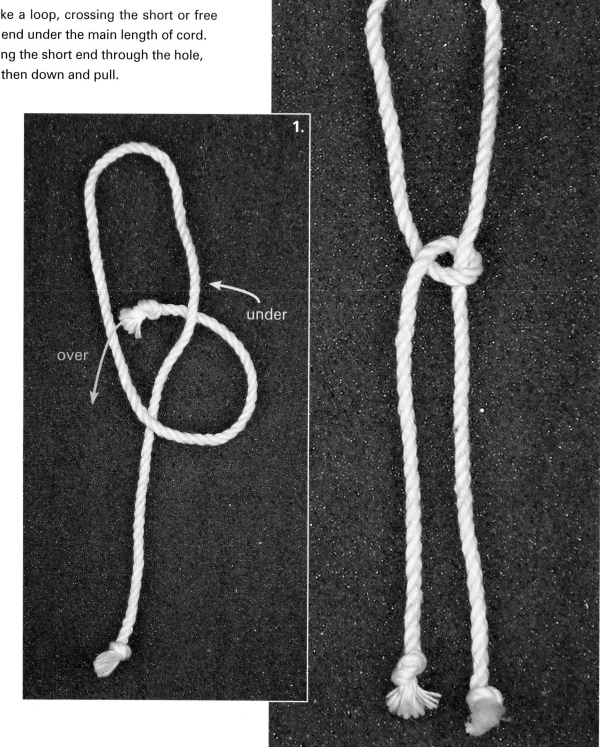

# Double Half Hitch

As the name implies, this knot is two half hitches, tied in sequence.

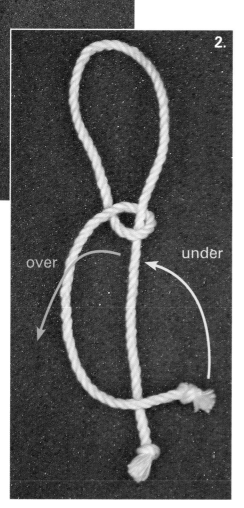

### Directions:

1. Make a loop, crossing the short or free end under the main length of cord, bringing the short end over and down through the hole.
2. For a second time, cross the short or free end under the main length of cord and down through the hole.
3. Tighten all portions to form the knot.

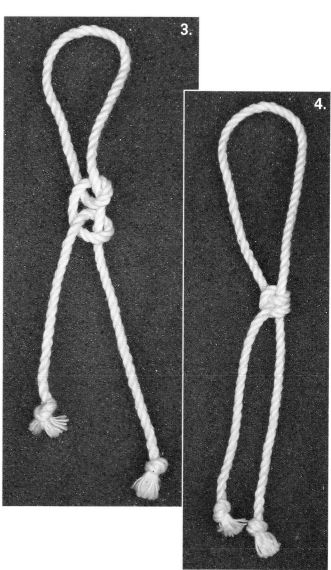

# Clove Hitch

A beautiful way to define and separate sections of your pattern.
The front side of the work will look almost like a horizontal line of beads.
On the back of your work, each clove hitch you make will look like a slash or backslash.

front

back

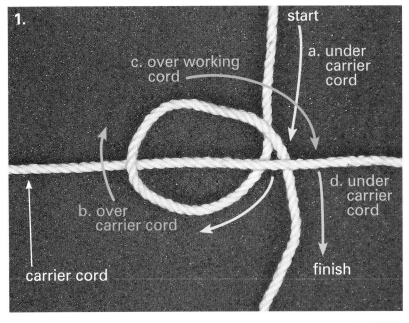

**1.**

start

a. under carrier cord

c. over working cord

d. under carrier cord

b. over carrier cord

carrier cord

finish

**2.**

## Directions:

1. Bring the loose end of the cord over a carrier cord, and slightly to the one side.
2. Tighten over the carrier cord.
3. Bring the loose end over the carrier cord a second time passing through the loop.
4. Tighten to completely form the knot.
5. On the reverse side, the cords will appear to form the letter X.

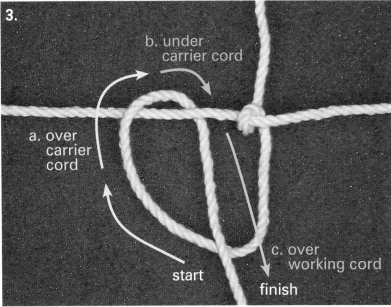

**3.**

b. under carrier cord

a. over carrier cord

c. over working cord

start

finish

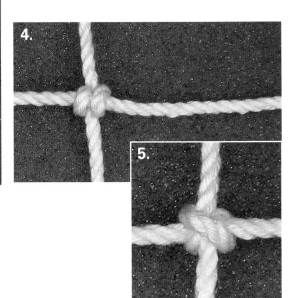

**4.**

**5.**

# Square Knot

This knot is one you have likely been tying for most of your life.

It the same knot used to tie your shoelace, but without the loops.

For stability, and to allow for a clean alternating pattern, it is frequently worked with two vertical carrier cords through the center.

Another common name is reef knot.

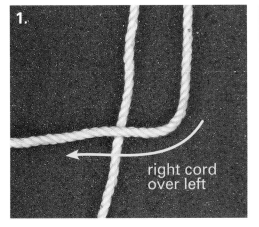

1.

right cord over left

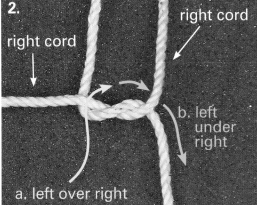

2.

right cord

right cord

b. left under right

a. left over right

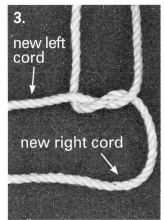

3.

new left cord

new right cord

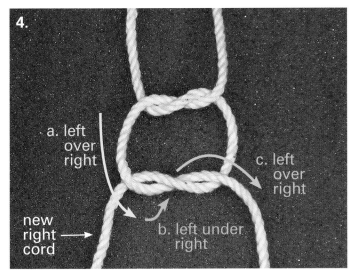

4.

a. left over right

c. left over right

new right cord →

b. left under right

5.

## Directions:

1. Beginning with two cords, bring the right cord across toward the left.
2. Wrap the left cord over the right cord, then through to the back.
3. Bring the new right cord across.
4. Wrap the left cord under the right cord, then through to the front.
5. Pull the ends evenly to form a symmetrical knot.

# Crown Sinnet

Also called the lanyard knot or box stitch, you might remember making key rings and lanyards with this knot using flat plastic lacing.

A great starting point the bottom center of a three dimensional project because it has a neat appearance, and provides four mounting cords from which you can expand the circumference.

front

back

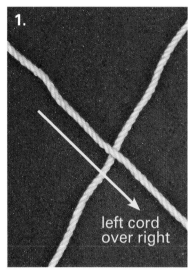
1.

left cord over right

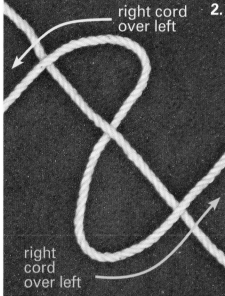
2.

right cord over left

right cord over left

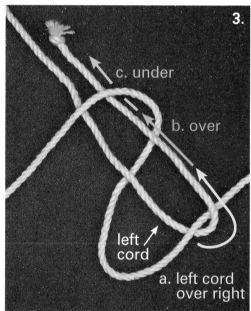
3.

c. under

b. over

left cord

a. left cord over right

## Directions:

1. Start by laying the two cords across each other at their centers.
2. Cross ends of the bottom cord across the top cord to form a letter S.
3. Tuck one free end of the top cord under the loop of the S.
4. Tuck the other free end of the top cord under the other loop of the S.
5. Pull all four strands evenly for a symmetrical final knot.
6. The reverse side of the knot will appear to form a letter X.

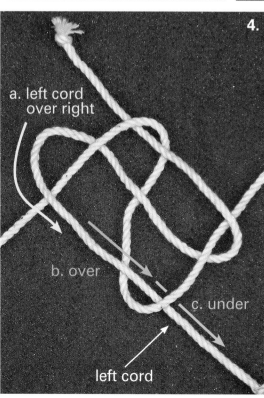
4.

a. left cord over right

b. over

c. under

left cord

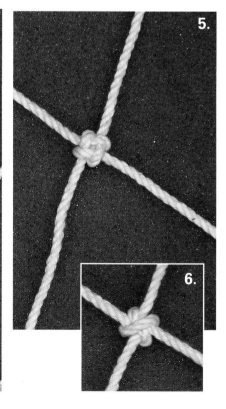
5.

6.

*6*

*Beginner Projects*

## Diamond Square Belt

### Preparation:

Finished belt measures 62 inches long

(26 inches knotted, plus 18 inches of fringe tie at each end).

You'll need at least 128 feet of 3 mm waxed cotton cord.

Measure and cut sixteen cords that are 96 inches each in length.

Tie off each end of each cord with an overhand knot to prevent fraying.

Pinning the work to a board or pillow can make it easier to keep this pattern uniform.

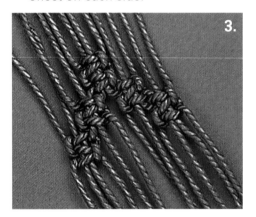

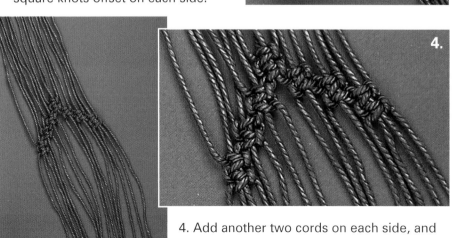

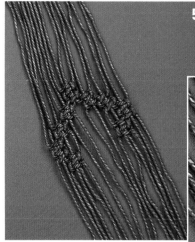

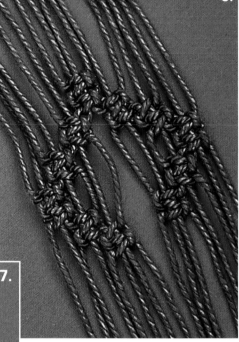

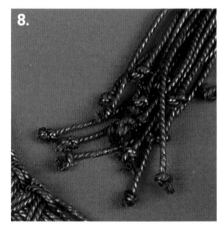

1. Tie two square knots in the middle four cords.

2. Now add two cords to each side and tie one and one-half square knots offset on each side.

3. Add two more cords to each side, and again tie one and one-half square knots offset on each side.

4. Add another two cords on each side, and tie two square knots offset on each side.

5. Skip two cords on each side, and tie one and one-half square knots offset on each side.

6. Again skip two cords on each side, and tie one and one-half square knots offset on each side.

7. Repeat step 1 through step 6 eight times, tie two square knots in the middle four cords, then finish with double-stranded square knots to gather the cords at each end.

8. Trim ends to even them out, and tie additional overhand knots as needed. Fasten the belt by tying the cords at each end together into one square knot.

# Diamond Square Scarf

## Preparation:

Finished scarf measures 62 inches long by 4
inches wide
(52 inches knotted, plus 3 inches of fringe at
each end).

You'll need at least 320 feet of worsted weight
acrylic yarn.

Choose a yarn that has resilient body, and that
knotting does not reduce the diameter of the
yarn significantly.

Measure and cut twenty cords that are 192 inches
each in length.

Tie off each end of each cord with an overhand
knot
to prevent fraying.

Pinning the work to a board or pillow can make
it easier to keep this pattern uniform.

## ←——— See illustrations for the Diamond Square Belt opposite

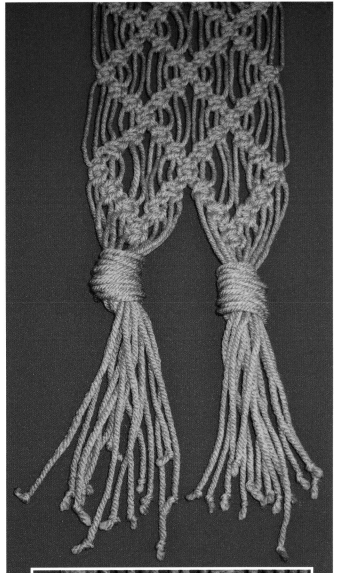

## Directions:

1. Arrange all yarns vertically on your work
   surface.
2. Skip six yarns and, in the next four yarns, tie
   two square knots.
3. Skip eight yarns and, in the next four yarns, tie
   two square knots.
4. Skip the six yarns that remain.
5. Tie one and one-half square knots offset beneath
   each square knot.
6. Again tie one and one-half square knots offset
   beneath each square knot.
7. Tie two square knots offset beneath each square
   knot, and you will now have involved all of the
   yarns.
8. Tie one and one-half square knots offset beneath
   each square knot.
9. Again tie one and one-half square knots offset
   beneath each square knot.
10. Repeat step 2 through step 9 sixteen times.
11. Divide yarns at each end into three even
    sections.

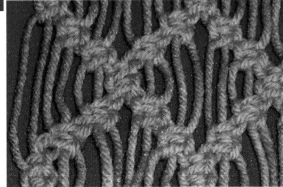

12. Finish with double-stranded square knots to
    gather the yarns at each end.
13. Trim ends to even them out, and tie additional
    overhand knots as needed.
14. If the movement of the first wearing causes
    the final knots to lose shape, you will find an
    appropriate fluid stitch or fray stop on the
    notion aisle of your local craft or fabric store.

*Intermediate Projects*

## Colorful Bracelet

### Preparation:

Finished bracelet measures approximately 8-1/2 inches between first square knots and last overhand knots.

You'll need at least 15 feet of each of two compatible colors of 1 mm waxed cotton cord.

Cut two 90 inch cords of each color, resulting in four total strands.

Tie overhand knots in each end to ensure the cord does not fray as you work.

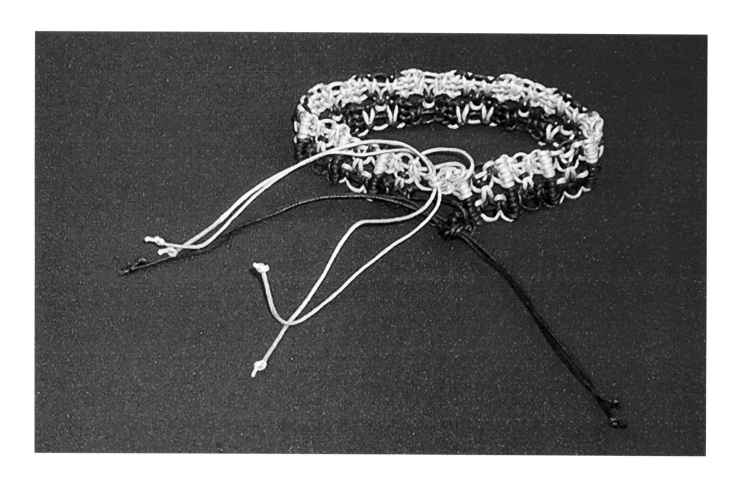

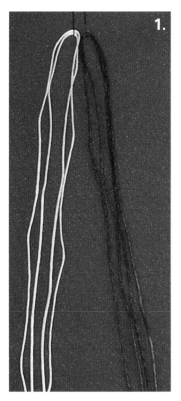

1. Make a loop with two cords of each color.

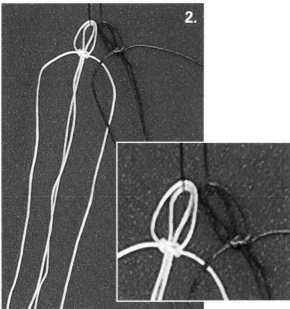

2. Tie a square knot in each loop.

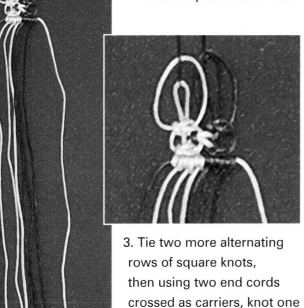

3. Tie two more alternating rows of square knots, then using two end cords crossed as carriers, knot one row of clove hitches.

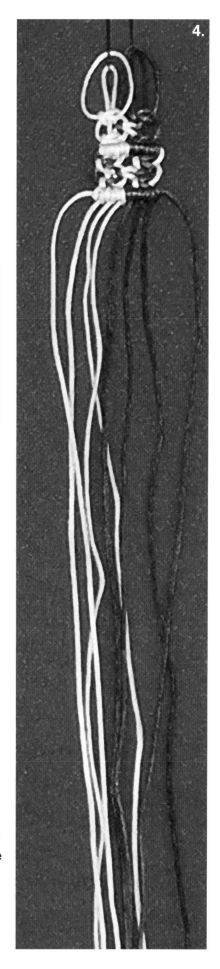

4. Repeat three rows of alternating square knots and a row of clove hitches thirteen times, resulting in fourteen sections.

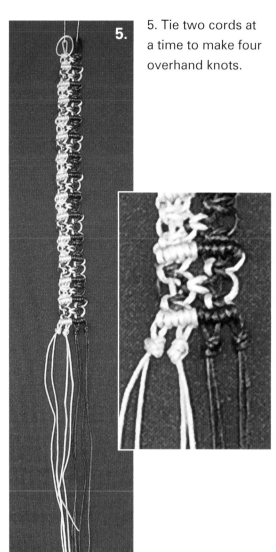

**5.** 5. Tie two cords at a time to make four overhand knots.

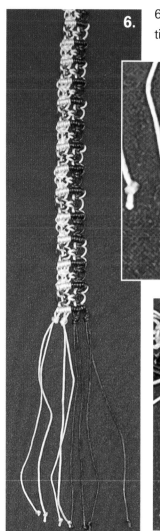

**6.** 6. Trim cords to match shortest length and tie overhand knots in the cut ends.

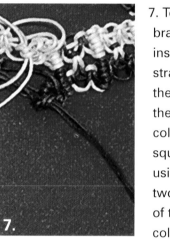

**7.** 7. To fasten bracelet, insert two strands into the loop of the same color, and tie square knot using other two strands of the same color.

# Matching Colorful Necklace

## Preparation:

Finished Necklace measures approximately 15 inches between first square knots and last overhand knots.

You'll need at least 29 feet of each of two compatible colors of 1 mm waxed cotton cord.

Cut two 174 inch cords of each color, resulting in four total strands.

Tie overhand knots in each end to ensure the cord does not fray as you work.

### See illustrations for the Colorful Bracelet on pages 27-28.

## Directions:

1. Make loop with two cords of each color.
2. Tie a square knot in each loop.
3. Tie two more alternating rows of square knots, then using two end cords crossed as carriers, knot one row of clove hitches.
4. Repeat three rows of alternating square knots and a row of clove hitches twenty-four times, resulting in twenty-five sections.
5. Tie two cords at a time to make four overhand knots.
6. Trim cords to match shortest length and tie overhand knots in the cut ends.
7. To fasten necklace, insert two strands into the loop of the same color, and tie square knot using other two strands of the same color.

# Looping Bracelet

## Preparation:

Finished bracelet measures approximately 9 inches between first and last overhand knots.

You'll need at least 9 feet of 2 mm waxed cotton cord.

And at least 9 feet of 1 mm faux leather cord.

Measure and cut two cords that are 54 inches each in length from each type of cord.

Tie off each end of each cord with an overhand knot to prevent fraying.

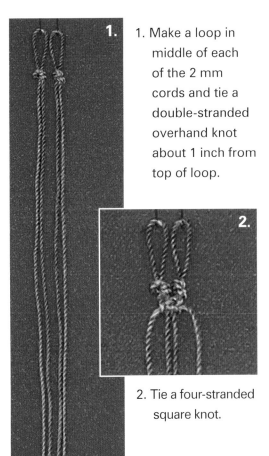

1.

1. Make a loop in middle of each of the 2 mm cords and tie a double-stranded overhand knot about 1 inch from top of loop.

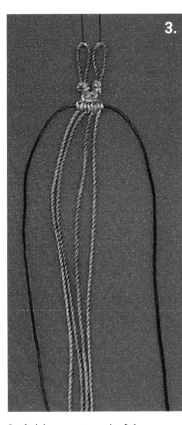

3.

2.

2. Tie a four-stranded square knot.

3. Add one strand of 1 mm cord as a carrier for a row of four clove hitches.

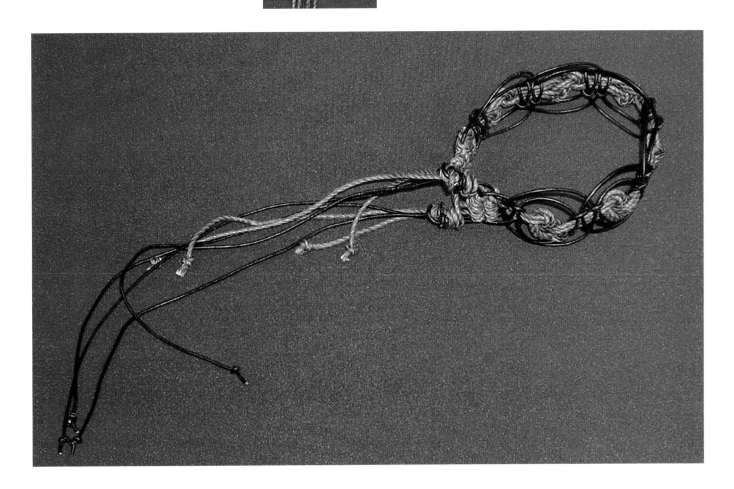

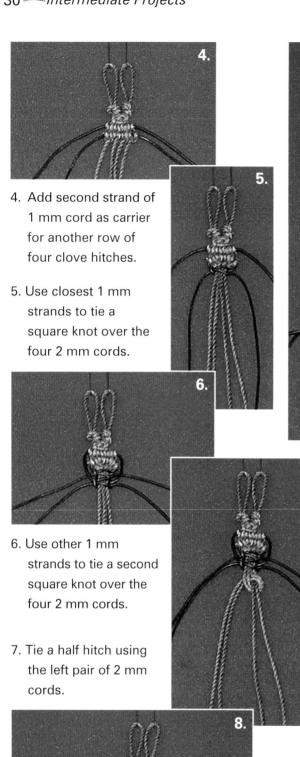

4. Add second strand of 1 mm cord as carrier for another row of four clove hitches.

5. Use closest 1 mm strands to tie a square knot over the four 2 mm cords.

6. Use other 1 mm strands to tie a second square knot over the four 2 mm cords.

7. Tie a half hitch using the left pair of 2 mm cords.

8. Tie another half hitch using the right pair of 2 mm cords.

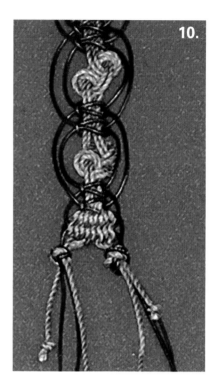

9. Repeat step 5 through step 8 five more times, resulting in a total of six sections.

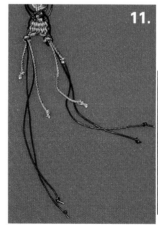

10. Repeat steps 5 and 6 once more then using two end cords crossed as carriers, knot two rows of clove hitches.

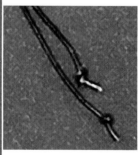

11. Gather four cords into each of two overhand knots.

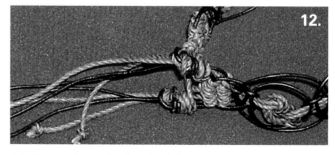

12. Fasten bracelet by doubling loop end over fringed end.

# Matching Looping Necklace

## Preparation:

Finished necklace measures approximately 15 inches between first and last overhand knots.

You'll need at least 22-1/2 feet of 2 mm waxed cotton cord.

And at least 22-1/2 feet of 1 mm faux leather cord.

Measure and cut two cords that are 135 inches each in length from each type of cord.

Tie off each end of each cord with an overhand knot to prevent fraying.

← **See illustrations for the Looping Bracelet on page 29-30.**

1. Make a loop in middle of each of the 2 mm cords and tie a double-stranded overhand knot about 1 inch from top of loop.
2. Tie a four-stranded square knot.
3. Add one strand of 1 mm cord as a carrier for a row of four clove hitches.
4. Add second strand of 1 mm cord as carrier for another row of four clove hitches.
5. Use closest 1 mm strands to tie a square knot over the four 2 mm cords.
6. Use other 1 mm strands to tie a second square knot over the four 2 mm cords.
7. Tie a half hitch using the left pair of 2 mm cords.
8. Tie another half hitch using the right pair of 2 mm cords.
9. Repeat step 5 through step 8 from above fourteen more times, resulting in a total of fifteen sections.
10. Repeat steps 5 and 6 once more from above.
11. Gather four cords into each of two overhand knots.
12. Fasten necklace by doubling loop end over fringed end.

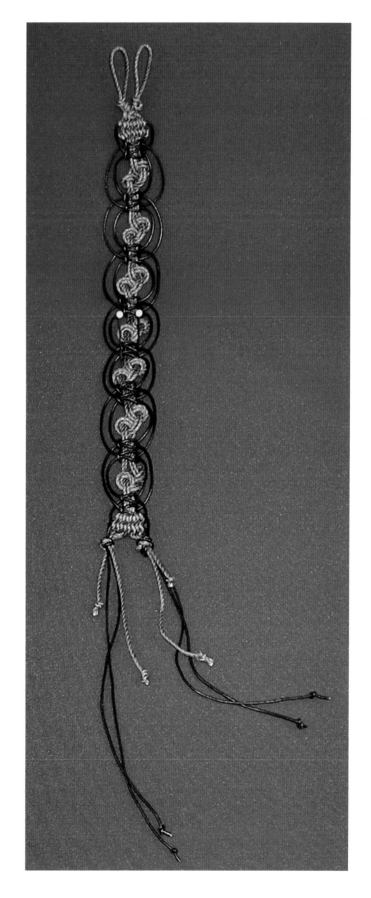

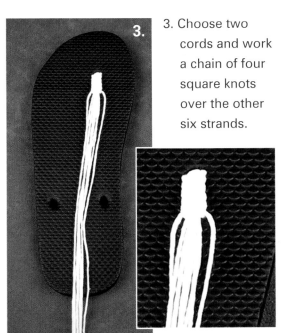

# Sandal T-Straps

## Preparation:

Sandal bases shown are readily available through craft stores, and discounters.

If preferred, cork or wooden sandal bases can generally be ordered through your local shoe repair shop.

You'll need at least 80 feet of 2 mm 10 ply cotton machine or kitchen twine.

Measure and cut sixteen cords that are 60 inches each in length.

Tie overhand knots in the ends of all working cords so they do not fray.

1. Set aside eight cords to use later. Fold two sets of four cords in half, and tie one large overhand knot in each, close to the loop.

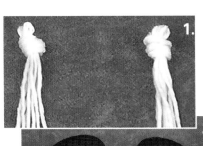

2. Insert loose ends though from the bottom of the hole at the front of the sandal. Take care to seat the knot completely within the hole, and flush with the bottom of the sandal.

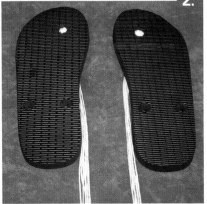

3. Choose two cords and work a chain of four square knots over the other six strands.

4. Select the four center cords and tie a square knot.

5. Cross every two cords and mount a lark's head on each cross.

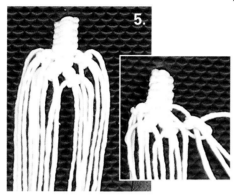

6. Cross the two end cords as carriers for a curved row of clove hitches.

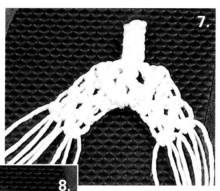

7. Begin each strap with five alternating rows of square knots.

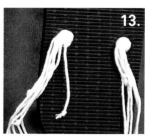

8. With the center four cords of each strap, knot a chain of three square knots.

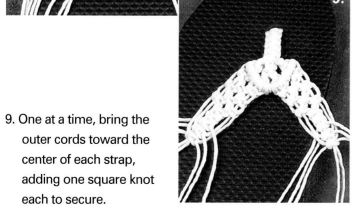

9. One at a time, bring the outer cords toward the center of each strap, adding one square knot each to secure.

10. Add two more square knots to the center of each chain.

11. On the straps toward the instep of each sandal, knot twelve (medium knot fourteen, large knot sixteen) alternating rows of square knots. On the outer straps of each sandal, knot fourteen (size medium knot sixteen, large knot eighteen) alternating rows of square knots.

12. Insert loose cords of each strap through hole toward bottom of sandal. Pull through just enough for end of knotting to be visible from the bottom.

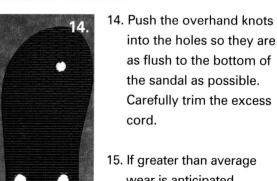

13. Gather all eight cords in each hole, and tie one large overhand knot in each as close to the end of the knot pattern as possible.

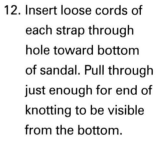

14. Push the overhand knots into the holes so they are as flush to the bottom of the sandal as possible. Carefully trim the excess cord.

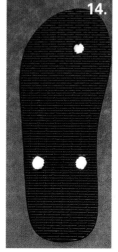

15. If greater than average wear is anticipated, consider adding a spot of glue to further secure each final knot. Otherwise, your sandals are ready to wear.

# Embellishment for Clothing

## Preparation:

The pattern for the Sandal T-Straps above has been adapted to embellish a v-neck tee shirt.

This pattern is based upon a neck opening that measures 10 inches from the bottom of the V to the shoulder seam, and 7 inches across from shoulder seam to shoulder seam, for a total of 27 inches.

You'll need at least 174 feet of 2 mm 10 ply cotton twine.

Measure and cut eight strands that are 260 inches each in length.

Tie overhand knots in the ends of all working strands so they do not fray.

## Directions:

1. Set aside four strands to use later. Fold four strands in half, and loop over pin on board.
2. Tie a four-stranded square knot.
3. Cross every two strands and mount a lark's head on each cross.
4. Cross the two end strands as carriers for a curved row of clove hitches.
5. Begin each section of the neck with five alternating rows of square knots.
6. With the center four strands of each section of the neck, knot a chain of three square knots.
7. One at a time, bring the outer cords toward the center of each section of the neck, adding one square knot each to secure.
8. Add two more square knots to the center of each chain.
9. On each section of the neck, knot five more alternating rows of square knots.
10. Repeat step 6 through step 9 six times.
11. Baste, or loosely sew, the work you have completed with the actual neck opening, and add or remove rows of alternating square knots to fit the opening exactly.
12. With a needle, pass the yarn ends through to the inside of the back of the neck.
13. Then pass the yarn ends through the shirt fabric and tie off with double overhand knots under

the basted embellishment and trim excess yarn close to the knots.

14. Working upward from the bottom of the neck opening, neatly sew the basted embellishment to the shirt.
15. Remove the basting stitches.

# Yoga Mat Harness

## Preparation:

Further adapting the base patterns above, you can create a useful harness to carry your yoga mat.

This pattern can accommodate a yoga mat that measures the average 12 inches to 24 inches in circumference when rolled.

You'll need at least 520 feet of 2 mm 10 ply cotton machine or kitchen twine.

Measure and cut eight strands that are 260 inches each in length.

Tie overhand knots in the ends of all working strands so they do not fray.

## Directions:

1. Set aside four strands to use later. Fold four strands in half, and loop over pin on board.
2. Tie a four-stranded square knot.
3. Cross every two strands and mount a lark's head on each cross.
4. Cross the two end strands as carriers for a curved row of clove hitches.
5. Begin each section of the harness with five alternating rows of square knots.
6. With the center four strands of each section of the harness, knot a chain of three square knots.
7. One at a time, bring the outer cords toward the center of each section of the harness, adding one square knot to secure.
8. Add two more square knots to the center of each chain.
9. On each section of the harness, knot five more alternating rows of square knots.
10. Repeat step 6 through step 9 fourteen times, or until the length of each section of the harness reaches 41 inches.
11. Gather each section's cords into an overhand knot.
12. Trim ends evenly, and tie additional overhand knots in the ends as needed.
13. To harness your yoga mat, first lay your harness on the floor, then lay your yoga mat across the two end sections.
14. Tie each loose end around your yoga mat and secure with a double half hitch.

# Cell Phone Pouch

## Preparation:

This project fits a phone that measures up to 2-3/8 inches wide by 3-7/8 inches long x 5/8 inch in thickness.

Finished pouch measures 3-1/2 inches wide by 4-1/2 inches long by 1 inch thick excluding fringe, or 2-1/2 inches thick including fringe.

Finished strap measures 21 inches long from top overhand knot to top of pouch.

You'll need at least 217 feet of 3 mm cotton cable cord.

For a dressier look, substitute 3 mm waxed cotton cord in any color.

Measure and cut twenty cords that are 130 inches each in length.

Tie overhand knots in the ends of all working cords so they do not fray.

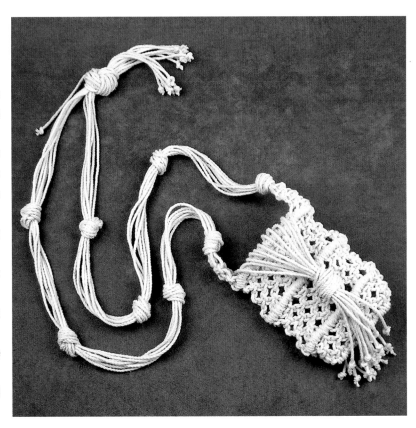

1. Set aside four cords to use later, and mount a row of fifteen lark's head knots in alternating directions upon the center of the sixteenth cord.

2. Knot two alternating rows of square knots in each direction.

3. Cross the end cords from first row of square knots and mount two lark's head knots on each cross.

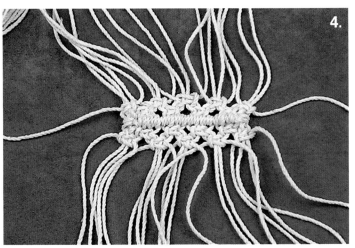

4. Bend the work slightly at the first line of lark's head knots, and work two square knots at each end, resulting in 5 square knots across each side.

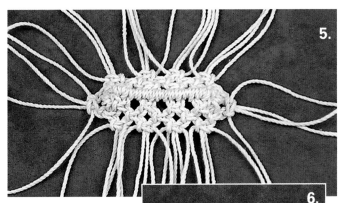

5.

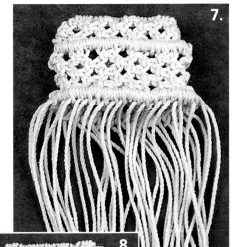

6.

5. Now fold the work completely in half and work an entire row of square knots to fan out a bit as you work to keep the tension loose.

6. Choose one cord from middle of the square knot on each end, and cross to form a carrier on one side of the pouch. Knot one clove hitch plus one half hitch with each cord across the carrier. Repeat for other side of pouch. Then knot five alternating rows of square knots around the entire pouch.

7. Again, choose one cord from middle of the square knot on each end, and cross to form a carrier on one side of the pouch. Knot one clove hitch plus one half hitch with each cord across the carrier. Repeat for other side of pouch.

7.

8. Tie five more alternating rows of square knots around the entire pouch.

8.

9.

9. For a third time, choose one cord from middle of the square knot on each end, and cross to form a carrier on one side of the pouch. Knot one clove hitch plus one half hitch with each cord across the carrier. Repeat for other side of pouch.

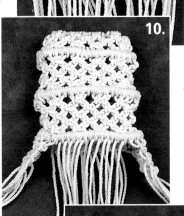

10.

10. Select the 8 cords at each corner and knot 5 rows of alternating square knots to begin the straps.

11.

11. Gather cords of each strap into an overhand knot. Repeat the overhand knots four times on each strap at regular intervals.

12.

12.

12. Gather both ends of strap into one large overhand knot. Gather working cords from each side of pouch into an overhand knot to form a decorative fringe. Trim all cords of the strap and fringe, and finish with additional overhand knots in the ends as needed.

## Creative Gallery

## The Contemporary Knotted Artwork of Darlyn Susan Yee

*Knotty Tree*, 1999.
Knotted Cotton, Polymer, Acrylic,
Plastic and Stone,
69" x 32" x 32".

The cotton string was first
knotted, then random coats of
polymer and acrylic were applied
to accentuate visual texture.

*Knothead*, 2000.
Knotted Cotton, Polyester and Stone, 13″ x 9″ x 10″.

Worked as a demonstration piece through the course of
a year, audiences of varied backgrounds expressed that
this piece looked just like one of their relatives.

*Knotted Vessel*, 2003.
Knotted Cotton, 14″ x 7″ x 7″.

Manipulation of the medium to balance
form, design and structure.

*Does Knot Hold Water I*, 2002.
Knotted Cotton, 10-1/2″ x 7-1/2″ x 7-1/2″.
*Private Collection of Cathey Cadieux.*

The tension used in the knotting process and that
of the knot patterns encouraged the contoured shape.

*Flourish*, 2009.
Knotted Cotton, 4-3/4″ x 8″ x 8″.

The methodical structure beneath blossoms,
opening to further possibilities.

*Tying The Knot*, 2008.
Hand Knotted Cotton
Wedding Dress Installation,
70″ x 32″ x 48″.

Displayed as a work in
progress to represent that
being a bride is not the end
result we perceive as children.
In healthy relationships, we
allow ourselves continued
growth.

*Undercurrent*, 2009.

Knotted Cotton, 5″ x 6-1/2″ x 6-1/2″.
A vessel reflecting conscious
movement of the pattern of the
fiber in opposite directions.

*Excessively Handled*, 2007.

Knotted Cotton, 13-1/2″ x 8-1/2″ x 8-1/2″.
Not only does this vessel have
too many handles, it also has been
excessively handled while tying
over 10,000 knots to form it.

*Does Knot Hold Water III*, 2003.

Knotted Cotton, 11-1/2″ x 7″ x 7″.
Working multiple tendrils or sections
simultaneously resulted in the intricate
elbow pattern at the top of this vessel.

*Loopy*, 2005.

Knotted Cotton, 14-1/2″ x 8″ x 8″.
Opportunities to shape and construct
are presented by the use of fiber
that are almost impossible to
execute with any other material.

*Sunny Disposition*, 2005.
Knotted Cotton and Stone,
22″ x 3-1/2″ x 3-1/2″.

A wave of the scepter will bring
happiness and sunshine.

*All In It Together*, 2005.
Knotted Cotton and Stone,
10″ x 6″ x 6″.

Eight figures working in unison
and supporting the column.

*Spiral Pillar*, 2001.
Knotted Cotton and Stone,
15-1/2″ x 7″ x 7″.

Initially intended to represent a
pillar of strength, this classic
form has also been interpreted
by viewers as a totem and a bullet.

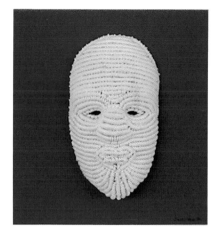

*Out Of The Blue*, 2009.
Knotted Cotton and Acrylic on Canvas,
12" x 4-1/2" x 4-1/2".

The face which springs forth from
the canvas is unexpected.

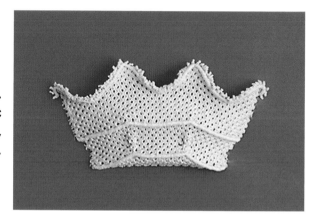

*Fluted Bowl*, 2009.
Knotted Cotton and Acrylic
on Canvas,
24" x 36" x 5".

*Regal Urn*, 2009.
Knotted Cotton and Acrylic on Canvas,
20" x 16" x 6-1/2".

A classic form reinterpreted into
a contemporary context.

*Reef*, 2009.
Knotted Cotton and Acrylic on Canvas,
16" x 20" x 4".

This reef knot is constructed
of many other reef knots.

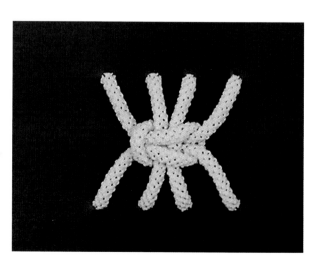

*Night Sky*, 2009.
Knotted Cotton and Acrylic on Canvas,
30" x 40" x 8".

Every few years, the oscillating orbits of
Mars and Earth bring them close enough
together to create the illusion of another
planet that resembles the Moon.

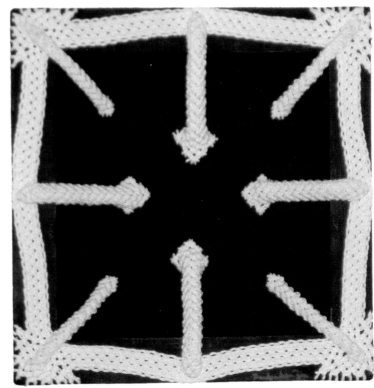

*Fourth Wall,* 2008.
Knotted Cotton and Acrylic on Canvas,
12" x 12" x 2".

The tendrils reaching into the darkness are
reminiscent of an actors attempts to reach
beyond the stage to an audience.

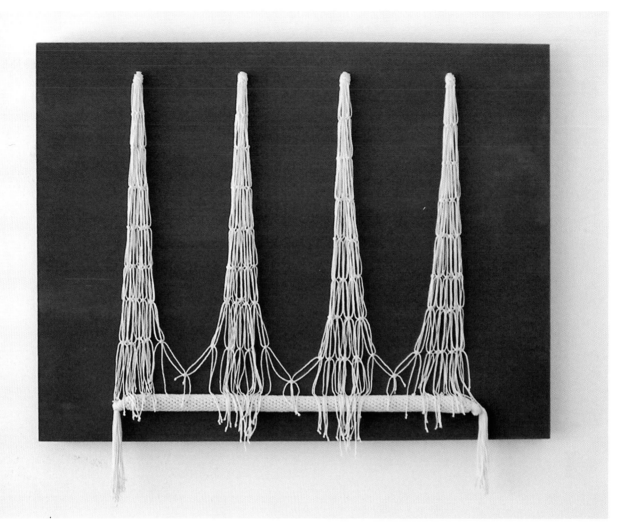

*Flow*, 2009.
Knotted Cotton and Acrylic on Canvas,
30″ x 40″ x 4″.

*Grow*, 2009.
Knotted Cotton and Acrylic on Canvas,
40″ x 30″ x 6-1/2″.

The delicate flower has a mind of its own
and appears to be dancing on the canvas.

# Selected Bibliography

elow are the reference sources used directly in the preparation of this book. It is neither a complete record of the books read since the first knot was tied, nor a record of all websites available now.

Some of the books are out of print. Combine renewed interest in knotting with a trend toward digital reproductions and you might find accessing them easier as you read than at the time of this writing.

Alfers, Betty. *Macramé*. New York, New York: Grosset & Dunlap, 1971.

Ashley, Clifford W. *The Ashley Book of Knots*. Garden City, New York: Doubleday & Company, Inc., 1967.

de Dillmont, Thérèse. *Encyclopedia of Needlework*. Philadelphia, Pennsylvania: Courage Books, and Imprint of Running Press Book Publishers, 1996.

Griswold, Lester. *Handicraft: Simplified Procedure and Projects*. Colorado Springs, Colorado: Lester Griswold, 1942

International Guild of Knot Tyers. *Knot Charts*. Wirral, United Kingdom: International Guild of Knot Tyers. accessed 2010. http://www.igkt.net/pdf/KnotChartsWeb.pdf

Lambert, Patricia, Barbara Staepelaere, and Mary G. Fry. *Color and Fiber*. West Chester, Pennsylvania: Schiffer Publishing Ltd., 1986.

Leslie, Catherine Amoroso. *Needlework Through History: An Encyclopedia (Handicrafts Through World History)*. Santa Barbara, California: Greenwood Press, 2007

Meilach, Dona Z. *A Modern Approach to Basketry with Fibers and Grasses*. New York, New York: Crown Publishers, Inc., 1974

Metropolitan Museum of Art. *Heilbrunn Timeline of Art History*. New York, New York: Metropolitan Museum of Art, accessed 2010. http://www.metmuseum.org/toah/

Museum of Arts and Design, New York. "Browse the Collection." Accessed 2010 at http://collections.madmuseum.org/code/emuseum.asp?emu_action=quicksearch

Print Free Graph Paper. *Print Free Graph Paper*. Anchorage, Alazka: Print Free Graph Paper, accessed 2010. http://www.printfreegraphpaper.com/

Skinner, Tina. *100 Artists of the West Coast II*. Atglen, Pennsylvania: Schiffer Publishing Ltd., 2009.

Smithsonian American Art Museum. *Search Collections*. Washington, DC: Smithsonian American Art Museum, accessed 2010. http://americanart.si.edu/collections/search/

Sunset Books and Sunset Magazine. *Macramé: Creative Knot-Tying Techniques*. Menlo Park, California: Lane Books, 1973.

Vertex42, LLC. *Free Printable Graph Paper*. Provo, Utah: Vertex42 LLC, accessed 2010. http://www.vertex42.com/ExcelTemplates/graph-paper.html

*D*arlyn Susan Yee is a self-trained fiber and mixed media artist living and working in Los Angeles, California. She celebrates the cultural significance of traditional fiber methods and their influence on contemporary art. Throughout history, fiber and textile methods have become synonymous with the cultures they represent. Yee's consuming passion is the aspect of each tiny detail interacting with the others to form a whole.

Although she has been creating work in various media since childhood, in recent years Yee has been most stimulated by the textures that the knotting process yields. She hand-builds each artwork knot by knot, just as one would shape or form a clay object. Utilizing the knot structures and fiber properties, Yee encourages the final shape of each unique artwork.

Using techniques that were once considered women's work or home arts, Yee creates pieces of museum quality fine art. Due to her contemporary approach to traditional technique, Yee's work has been shown in a wide range of galleries and museums. Her fiber sculptures and mixed media works have won numerous awards in local, national and international competitions. Yee has also been included in the Schiffer book, *100 Artists of the West Coast II*, by Tina Skinner.

In 2006, Yee received the Center for Cultural Innovation's Business Plan Award. She gained access to a mentor who guided her through the planning and analysis required to attain studio space in the greater Los Angeles area. She realized that goal in 2007, and has been happily working in her private studio creating larger scale projects, while continuing to expand her body of work.